The ABCs of Buddhism
If You Want to Be Happy, Focus on Giving

The ABCs of Buddhism

*If You Want to Be Happy,
Focus on Giving*

By Hisashi Ota
Supervised by Kentaro Ito
Translated by Juliet Winters Carpenter

The ABCs of Buddhism: If You Want to Be Happy, Focus on Giving
By Hisashi Ota
Published by Ichimannendo Publishing, Inc. (IPI)
970 West 190th Street, Suite 920, Torrance, California 90502
info@i-ipi.com   www.i-ipi.com
© 2016 by Hisashi Ota. All rights reserved.
Supervised by Kentaro Ito
Translated by Juliet Winters Carpenter

Cover design by Kazumi Endo
Photograph by amanaimages

First edition, June 2016
Printed in Japan
20 19 18 17 16   1 2 3 4 5 6 7 8 9 10

No part of this book may be reproduced in any form without permission from the publisher.

This book was originally published in Japanese by Ichimannendo Publishing Co. Ltd. under the title of *Manga de wakaru bukkyo nyumon*.
© 2011 by Hisashi Ota

Distributed in the United States and Canada by Atlas Books Distribution, a division of BookMasters, Inc.
30 Amberwood Parkway, Ashland, Ohio 44805
1-800-Booklog   www.atlasbooks.com

Distributed in Japan by Ichimannendo Publishing Co. Ltd.
2-4-5F Kanda-Ogawamachi, Chiyoda-ku, Tokyo 101-0052
info@10000nen.com   www.10000nen.com

Library of Congress Control Number: 2015960635
ISBN 978-0-9898477-2-8

ISBN 978-4-925253-98-7

Contents

Lesson 1 — **Precious Life**
Why a single human life outweighs the earth 1

Lesson 2 — **The Law of Cause and Effect (1):**
The Foundation of Buddhism
The principle that makes a happy future 13

Lesson 3 — **The Law of Cause and Effect (2):**
Own Causes, Own Effects
Don't hate people or hold grudges. 23

Lesson 4 — **The Law of Cause and Effect (3):**
Karmic Power
My own actions determine my future. 33

Lesson 5 — **The Law of Cause and Effect (4):**
Cause and Effect in the Three Worlds
The present is the key to the past and the future. 41

Lesson 6 — **Six Good Deeds (1):**
The Importance of Doing Good
What is a good deed? 51

Lesson 7 — **Six Good Deeds (2):**
Giving 1
A poor person's one light outshines
a millionaire's 10,000. 59

Lesson 8 — **Six Good Deeds (3):**
Giving 2—The Seven Types of Nonmaterial Giving
Even if you have no money or possessions to give,
you can still be generous. 67

Lesson 9 — **Six Good Deeds (4):**
Giving 3—The Three Fields
Choose the objects of your acts of giving. 77

Lesson 10 — **Six Good Deeds (5):**
Keeping Promises and Patience
Always keep your promises,
and keep your temper, too. 87

Lesson 11 — **Six Good Deeds (6):**
Effort, Self-Reflection, and Self-Cultivation
Persevere—try harder than anyone else. 97

Lesson 12 — **The Flower Festival—Buddha's Birthday**
The real meaning of "Only I am holy" 107

Lesson 13	**The Eight Sufferings (1)**
	Birth, aging, sickness, and death are inescapable. 117

Lesson 14	**The Eight Sufferings (2)**
	A world overflowing with love and hate 127

Lesson 15	**The Blind Passions**
	Why are temple bells struck 108 times on New Year's Eve? 135

Lesson 16	**Abusive Talk, Words That Kill**
	We mustn't hurt others with our words. 145

Lesson 17	**Ignorance (Envy)**
	The ugly mind that begrudges others their happiness and takes pleasure in their misfortune 157

Lesson 18	**Seven Kinds of Pride**
	Human beings can't get away from conceit. 167

Lesson 19	**Know Gratitude, Feel Gratitude, Show Gratitude**
	An ingrate is not to be trusted. 177

Lesson 20	**The Spirit of Benefiting Others First**
	Being kind to others leads to your own happiness. ... 189

Introducing the cast
Your merry classmates

Mr. Suzuki

He can teach you all kinds of things about Buddhism in great detail.

Ichiro

A lively, carefree kid with a hearty appetite, and the class clown.

Hikari

A diligent pupil, she is a cheerful, perky girl.

Naoki

An easygoing guy.

Masako

She loves fashion.

Tatsuki

A beacon of intelligence?

Lesson 1
Precious Life

Why a single human life outweighs the earth

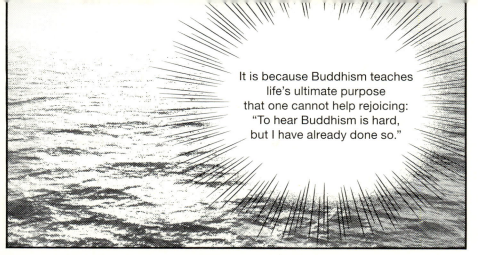

Lesson 2
The Law of Cause and Effect (1): The Foundation of Buddhism

The principle that makes a happy future

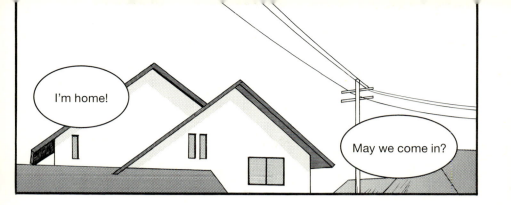

Lesson 3
The Law of Cause and Effect (2): Own Causes, Own Effects

Don't hate people or hold grudges.

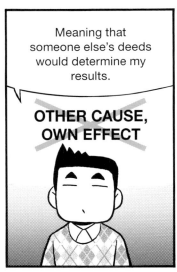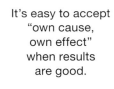

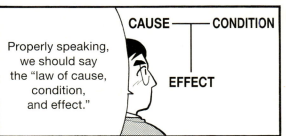
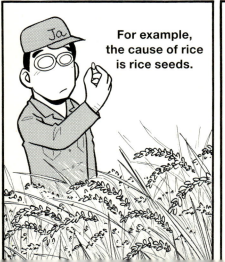
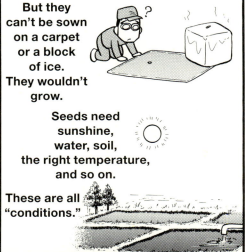

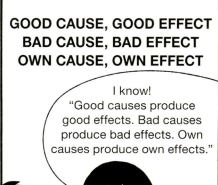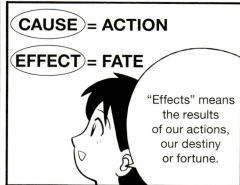

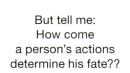

A scholar's brain can retain the contents of an entire library.

Holy smokes.

That doesn't mean his head is stuffed with actual books.

The contents are stored invisibly.

Right.

That reminds me of a poem!

Year after year cherry blossoms bloom again on Mt. Yoshino.
Split the tree and look inside—where are all the flowers?

Every spring, cherry blossoms come out on Mt. Yoshino.

But go there in winter, and there's nothing but withered-looking trees.

*Japanese Criminal Law Article 261 states that chopping another person's cherry tree constitutes property damage.

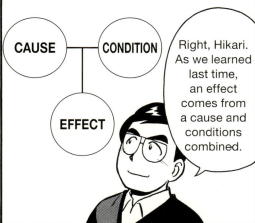

Lesson 5
The Law of Cause and Effect (4):
Cause and Effect in the Three Worlds

The present is the key to the past and the future.

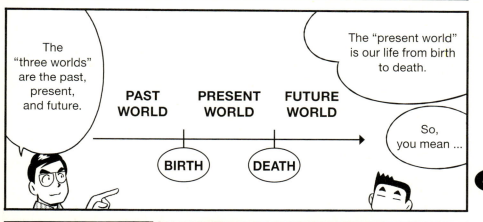

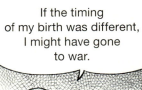

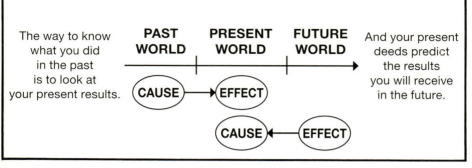

Lesson 6
Six Good Deeds (1): The Importance of Doing Good

What is a good deed?

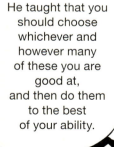

Lesson 7
Six Good Deeds (2): Giving 1

A poor person's one light outshines a millionaire's 10,000.

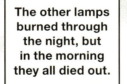

Lesson 8 Six Good Deeds (3): Giving 2—The Seven Types of Nonmaterial Giving

Even if you have no money or possessions to give, you can still be generous.

* A place to hear Buddhist sermons

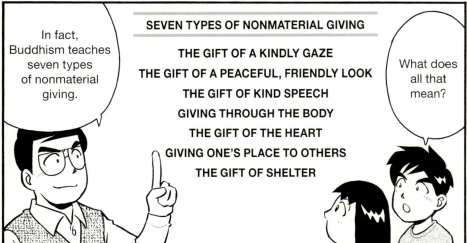

THE GIFT OF A KINDLY GAZE

Well, "the gift of a kindly gaze" means having a warm, gentle look in your eyes.

Huh. Can that be an act of giving?

Oh, right.

See? A kind look lifts the spirits of people around you and comforts people who are feeling down.

Ah, I feel better!

THE GIFT OF A PEACEFUL, FRIENDLY LOOK

"The gift of a peaceful, friendly look" means simply smiling.

Greeting others with a gentle smile is a wonderful form of giving!

GIVING THROUGH THE BODY

"Giving through the body" means doing physical labor for others or for society.

All right! I'll take on any muscle job!

Then rub my shoulders and back for me.

Uh, sure ...

THE GIFT OF THE HEART

"The gift of the heart" means saying heartfelt thanks.

Ah, right there! Wonderful. Thanks a lot!

It's nothing ...

"Giving one's place to others" means kindly giving up your place or seat.

GIVING ONE'S PLACE TO OTHERS

I always give my seat to old people on the train and bus!

Lesson 9
Six Good Deeds (4):
Giving 3 — The Three Fields

Choose the objects of your acts of giving.

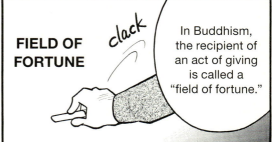

It means a field where good fortune grows.

Plant seeds in a field and a crop will soon grow, ripening into life-sustaining food.

In the same way, if we practice sincere acts of giving, we will definitely reap good results.

Right! A farmer planting seeds might think he's lost something because he gave up his seeds, but at harvest time he gets them back many times over!

So that's where the expression "field of fortune" comes from!

Buddha taught that there are three fields of fortune.

FIELD OF RESPECT
FIELD OF GRATITUDE
FIELD OF COMPASSION

These are called the "three fields."

Free fields?

No, "three fields."

Lesson 10 Six Good Deeds (5): Keeping Promises and Patience

Always keep your promises, and keep your temper, too.

Lesson 11
Six Good Deeds (6): Effort, Self-Reflection, and Self-Cultivation

Persevere—try harder than anyone else.

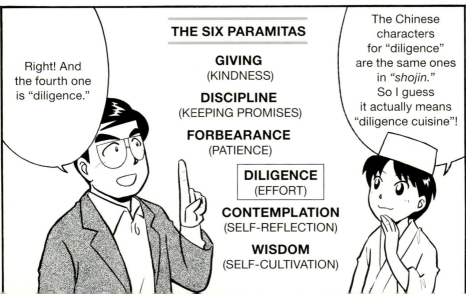

Lesson 12
The Flower Festival — Buddha's Birthday

The real meaning of "Only I am holy"

For once Naoki is running the show.

Yup, on April 8 about 2,600 years ago, he was born in a flower garden called Lumbini Park.

It was spring, and the park was full of flowers in glorious bloom!

That's why people came to celebrate Buddha's birthday with a Flower Festival.

Huh.

Now we know what the Flower Festival is! That's it for today.

FwuP

Time for cake!

Good grief. All you think about is food.

Wait, I just remembered.

BAP

There's a saying, "The mature rice plant lowers its head."

But actually he didn't say it to show how great he thinks he is. It means something else.

Truly great people act humble and respectful.

Right.

If that's true for ordinary people, it's even truer for Buddha!

Hmm ...

So what did he really mean?

Listen. The words "in heaven and earth" refer to the vastness of the universe!

ONLY

"Only" means "just." Only one.

Lesson 13
The Eight Sufferings (1)

Birth, aging, sickness, and death are inescapable.

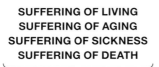

Lesson 14
The Eight Sufferings (2)

A world overflowing with love and hate

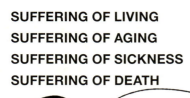

SUFFERING OF ENCOUNTERING THE DESPISED

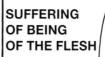

SUFFERING OF BEING OF THE FLESH

Lesson 15
The Blind Passions

Why are temple bells struck 108 times on New Year's Eve?

DESIRE FOR FOOD
DESIRE FOR WEALTH
DESIRE FOR LOVE
DESIRE FOR FAME
DESIRE FOR SLEEP

We desire food, wealth, love, fame, and sleep!

DESIRE FOR FOOD

The desire for food means the pleasure of eating.

Bring on the goodies!

Gourmet foods are in style. Everybody likes to eat.

DESIRE FOR WEALTH

Desire for wealth means the pleasure of accumulating money.

Money makes the world go 'round!

I want to make money, I don't want to lose a cent.

I study the ads to find the cheapest bargains!

But drive farther and end up spending more on gas?

Lesson 16
Abusive Talk, Words That Kill

We mustn't hurt others with our words.

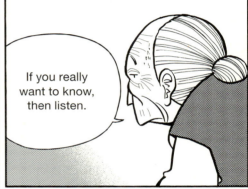

In my life I had many children, grandchildren, and great-grandchildren.

But death can come at any age, and some of them died before me. We have had 24 family funerals.

Each time, mourners in the next room would say the same thing—

What a shame it wasn't the old woman instead!!

They murmured it, but I heard.

Visitors talked behind my back, but my descendants said it to my face.

Every time, I was killed ...

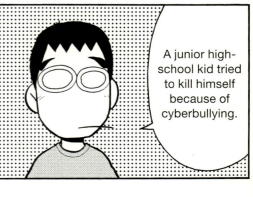

Lesson 17
Ignorance (Envy)

The ugly mind that begrudges others their happiness and takes pleasure in their misfortune

Lesson 18
Seven Kinds of Pride

Human beings can't get away from conceit.

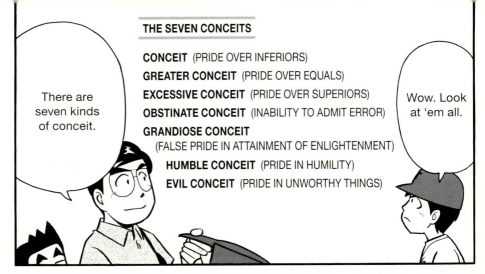

Lesson 19
Know Gratitude, Feel Gratitude, Show Gratitude

An ingrate is not to be trusted.

Lesson 20
The Spirit of Benefiting Others First

Being kind to others leads to your own happiness.

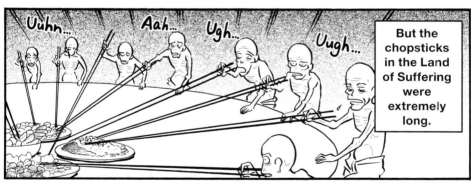

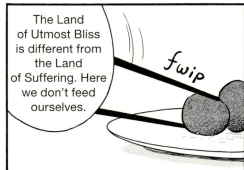

Afterword

Back when I was a child ... we lived in a world without cell phones or laptop computers. We kids would gather at a neighborhood temple for "Sunday school." Such chances are few today, when temples have largely become places for funerals and memorial services. With the change in values, now even funerals are held in abbreviated style, and more and more people go through life knowing little or nothing about Buddhism. This is extremely regrettable.

Buddhism, which our ancestors cared about so much that they held Sunday school to teach it to children, has much of importance to tell us about life itself. My desire to present the teachings of Buddha in a fashion that even small children could enjoy was the starting point for these comics. Rather to my surprise, adults have responded to the content even more enthusiastically than children, calling it easy to understand and enjoyable. This brought home to me the need for readily comprehensible books that explain Buddhism.

Nothing would make me happier than for people to take this book in hand and, perhaps with a few giggles along the way, learn the crucial teachings of Buddhism—teachings that can transform lives. It is especially gratifying to think that *The ABCs of Buddhism* will be accessible through this English translation to readers not only in Japan, but around the world. Those who want to know more about Buddha himself and what sort of person he was can refer to my book *The Story of Buddha: A Graphic Biography* (Ichimannendo Publishing, Inc., 2011). To anyone who would like to dig deeper and know the purpose of life, I recommend *You Were Born for a Reason* by Kentetsu Takamori, Daiji Akehashi, and Kentaro Ito (Ichimannendo Publishing, Inc., 2006).

My earnest desire is that the Buddhist teachings of salvation for one and all may bring happiness to all people on this earth.

Hisashi Ota
March 2016

Translator's Note

Buddhism began in India more than two millennia ago and has since spread through Asia and around the world. What's it all about? This book, based on the writings of Shinran (1173–1263), the founder of True Pure Land Buddhism in Japan, sets forth the teachings of Buddha in a style that children of all ages can understand and enjoy. I hope many children and their parents will join Ichiro and his friends on this rollicking adventure through *The ABCs of Buddhism* and beyond.

    I dedicate this translation with love to my grandchildren, Louise and Doris.

Juliet W. Carpenter
March 2016

• • About the Editorial Supervisor • •

KENTARO ITO
Born in Tokyo in 1969, he holds an M.A. in philosophy from the University of Tokyo. A philosopher and coauthor of *You Were Born for a Reason: The Real Purpose of Life* (Ichimannendo Publishing, Inc., 2006), he is also the author of *Otoko no tame no jibun-sagashi* [A man's journey of self-discovery], *Unmei o kirihiraku inga no hosoku* [The law of cause and effect that creates destiny], and other works.

• • About the Author • •

HISASHI OTA
Born in Shimane Prefecture in 1970, he graduated from Nagoya University's School of Science and Yoyogi Animation Academy. His other works include *The Story of Buddha: A Graphic Biography* (Ichimannendo Publishing, Inc., 2011) and *Manga rekishi jinbutsu ni manabu: Otona ni naru made ni mi ni tsuketai taisetsuna kokoro* [Learning from historical figures: Valuable lessons to take on board before adulthood—A comic] (Ichimannendo Publishing, Co. Ltd., 2016).

• • About the Translator • •

JULIET WINTERS CARPENTER
Born in Michigan in 1948, she studied Japanese language and literature at the University of Michigan. She has translated over 60 works, including *You Were Born for a Reason*, and has won numerous awards. She is the sole person to have received the Japan-U.S. Friendship Commission Prize for the Translation of Japanese Literature twice, in 1980 and again in 2015.

Other Titles from Ichimannendo Publishing, Inc.

List Price: US$16.95
248 pages/Paperback/
8.3×5.9 inches

THE STORY OF BUDDHA
A Graphic Biography

By Hisashi Ota
Supervised by Kentaro Ito

The Buddha's life story in illustration

What are we living for? Is there meaning to life? Some twenty-five hundred years ago, in his youth Buddha had the same nagging questions that we do today.
The search for the answer to these questions is the starting point of Buddhism.
In our desire to live with strength and goodwill, the life of Buddha provides invaluable insight and guidance.

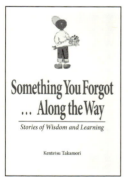

List Price: US$11.95
192 pages/Paperback/
7.4×5.1 inches

Something You Forgot ... Along the Way
Stories of Wisdom and Learning

By Kentetsu Takamori

This book introduces sixty-five heart-warming stories that show what it means to learn from life's events. These simple yet beautiful tales invite us to look deeper into almost any situation in life. In the tradition of Aesop's Fables, each story concludes with a moral lesson.
This book was originally published in Japanese by Ichimannendo Publishing Co. Ltd. It is part of a Japanese series that has sold over a million copies.

---

* "Ichimannen" means "ten thousand years" in Japanese and reflects the company's desire to publish books that will be cherished by readers well into the future.

Other Titles from Ichimannendo Publishing, Inc.

YOU WERE BORN FOR A REASON
The Real Purpose of Life

By Kentetsu Takamori, Daiji Akehashi, and Kentaro Ito

What is the meaning of life?

Where can we find true happiness that will never fade away?

What is there in life that will never betray us, that we can devote ourselves to without regret?

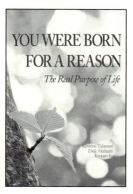

List Price: US$16.95
236 pages/Hardcover/
9.3×6.3 inches

These age-old questions cry out for clear answers—and this book addresses them head-on through the words of the revolutionary monk Shinran.

From the text:

"Without lasting joy or fulfillment in living, the days merge into one indistinguishable blur of eating, sleeping, and getting up. Living such a life is like running a footrace with no goal."

"French writer Albert Camus said that deep in the human heart is a 'wild longing' to know the meaning of life. We want to know, indeed we must know the meaning of life if we are to go on living."

"Once life's true purpose is known, all trouble and suffering acquires meaning. Live for life's true purpose, and all your efforts are sure to be rewarded."

★ ★ ★

YOU WERE BORN FOR A REASON is the English translation of the best-selling Japanese book on Buddhism, *Naze Ikiru,* which means "Why We Live."

You will not be the same after reading this book.

Other Titles from Ichimannendo Publishing, Inc.

List Price: US$30.00
144 pages/Hardcover/
10 x 7 inches

UNLOCKING TANNISHO
Shinran's Words on the Pure Land Path

By Kentetsu Takamori

Tannisho (Lamenting the Deviations) clarifies the heart of Pure Land Buddhism and points the way to real happiness with unforgettable expressions.
UNLOCKING TANNISHO is the only definitive commentary of this beloved classic text, and has been a remarkable success with almost a quarter of a million copies sold to date.

List Price: US$14.95
216 pages/Paperback/
7.4×5.1 inches

Unshakable Spirit
Stories of Compassion and Wisdom

By Kentetsu Takamori

Why wasn't there any rioting or looting in Japan after the devastating earthquake and tsunami of 2011?
Unshakable Spirit is a collection of heartwarming stories in which you will discover the Japanese people's underlying philosophy.

List Price: US$12.95
224 pages/Paperback/
7.4×5.1 inches

If you plant seeds of happiness, flowers of happiness will bloom

By Kazushi Okamoto

It's doing the little things today that makes your tomorrows brighter

Just as seeds cause flowers to bloom and fruit to appear, so our actions give rise to happiness or unhappiness. If we don't sow the seeds of happiness, we will never become happy. What are the seeds of happiness? This book guides the reader with clear and simple answers to this question.